Wonderful Christmas Coloring Books
Coloring Books For Kids

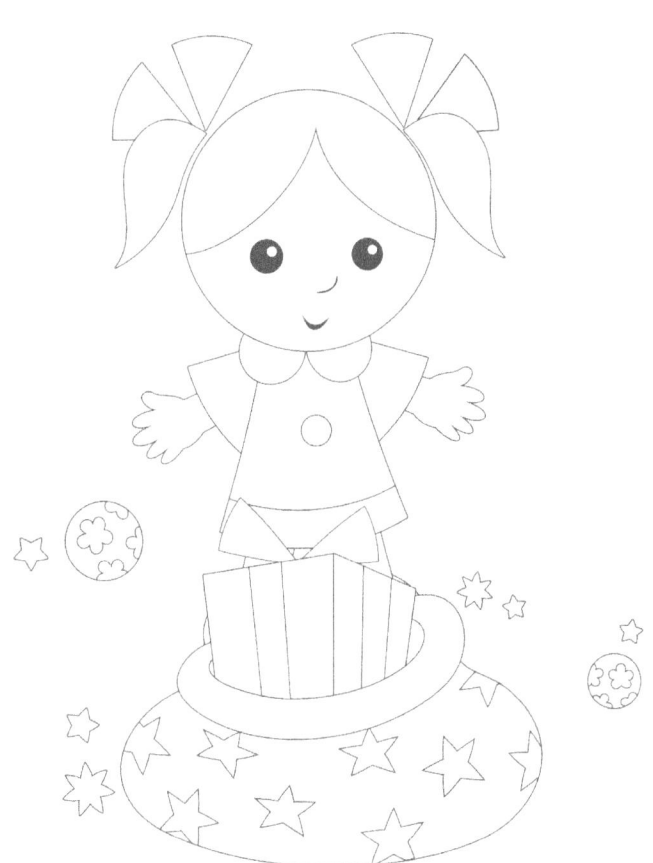

By
My Kids Coloring Books

Published by PUBLISHING COMPANY in 2015
First edition: First printing
Illustrations and design © 2015 My Kids Coloring Books

allcoloringbook.com

ISBN 978- 1517313883

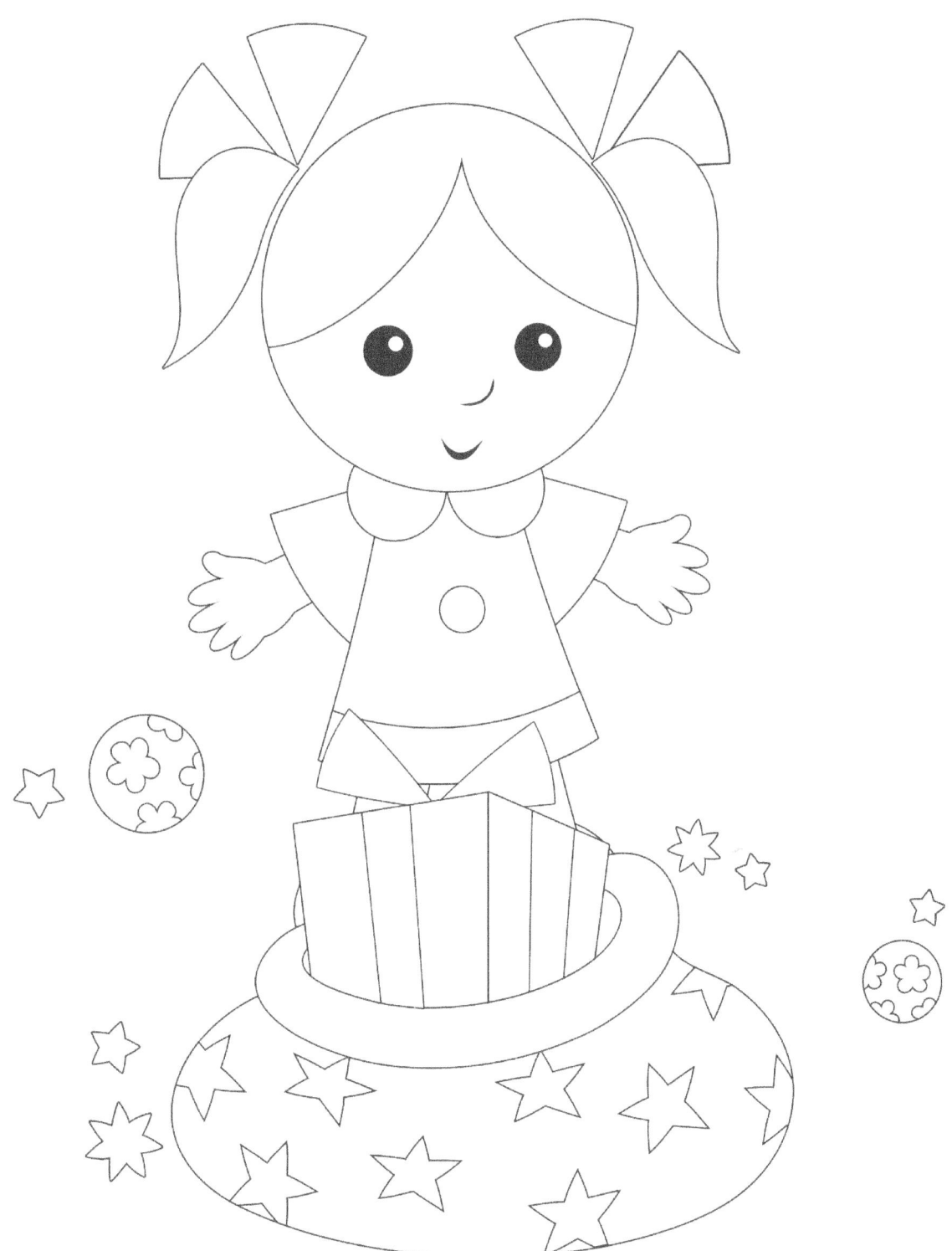

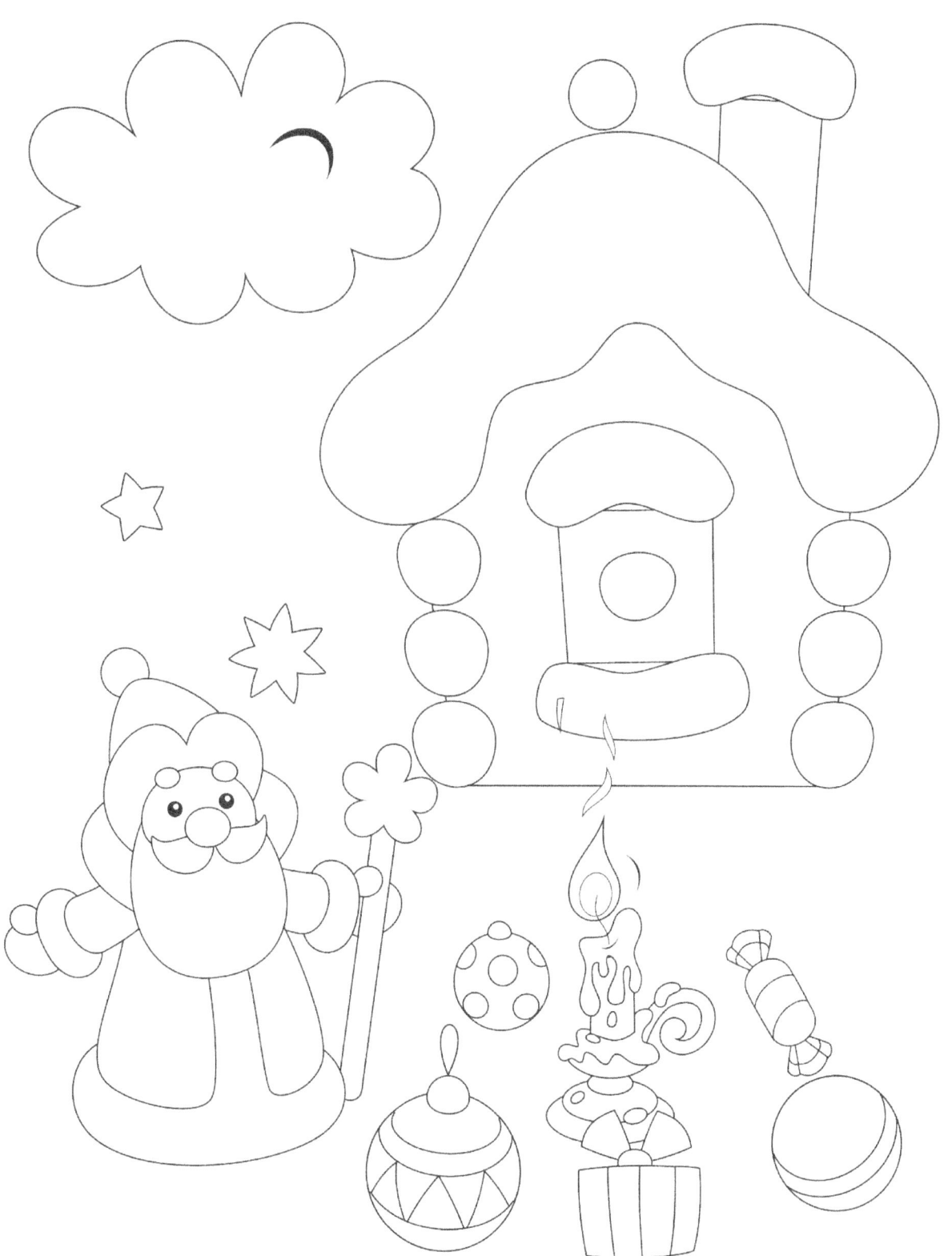

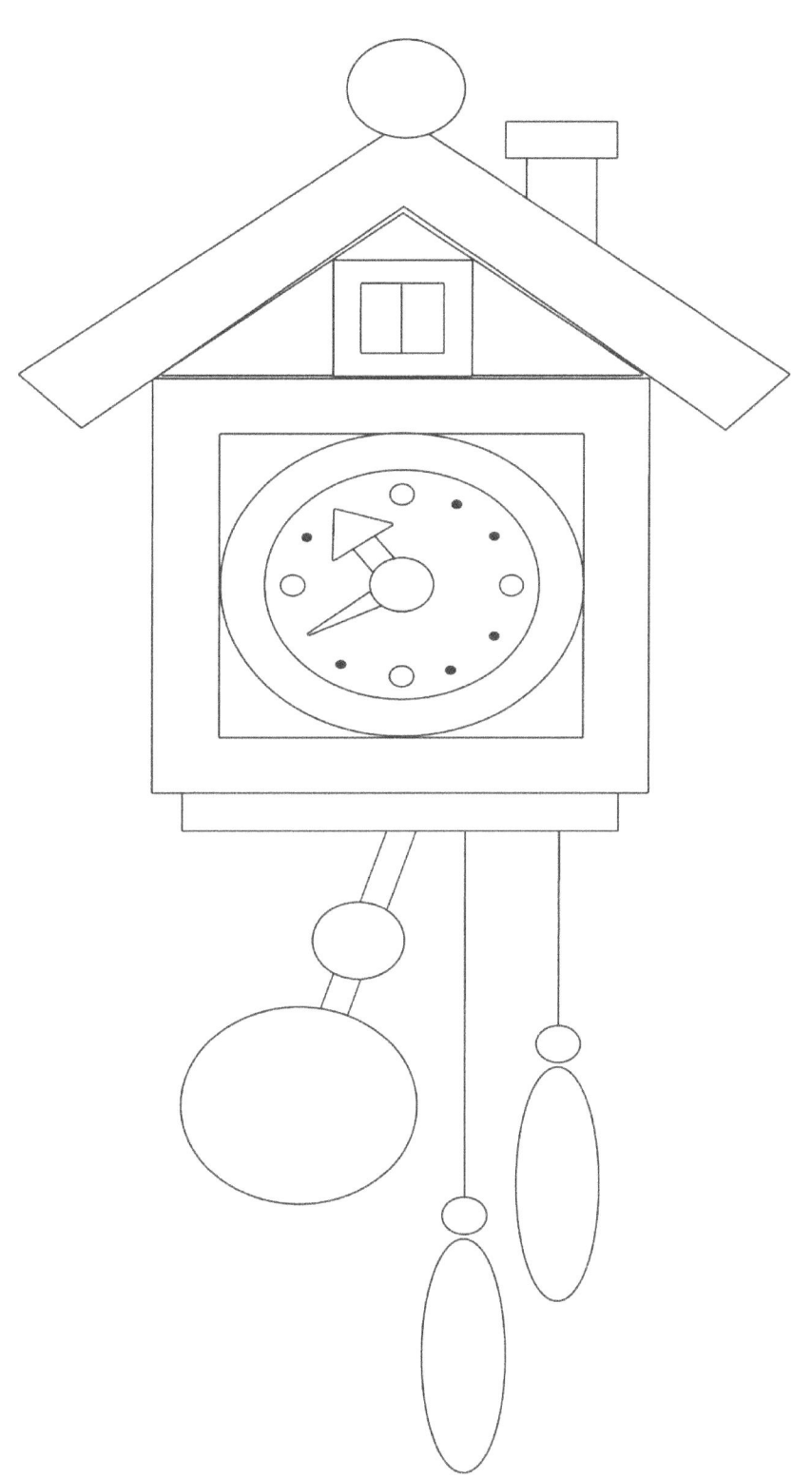

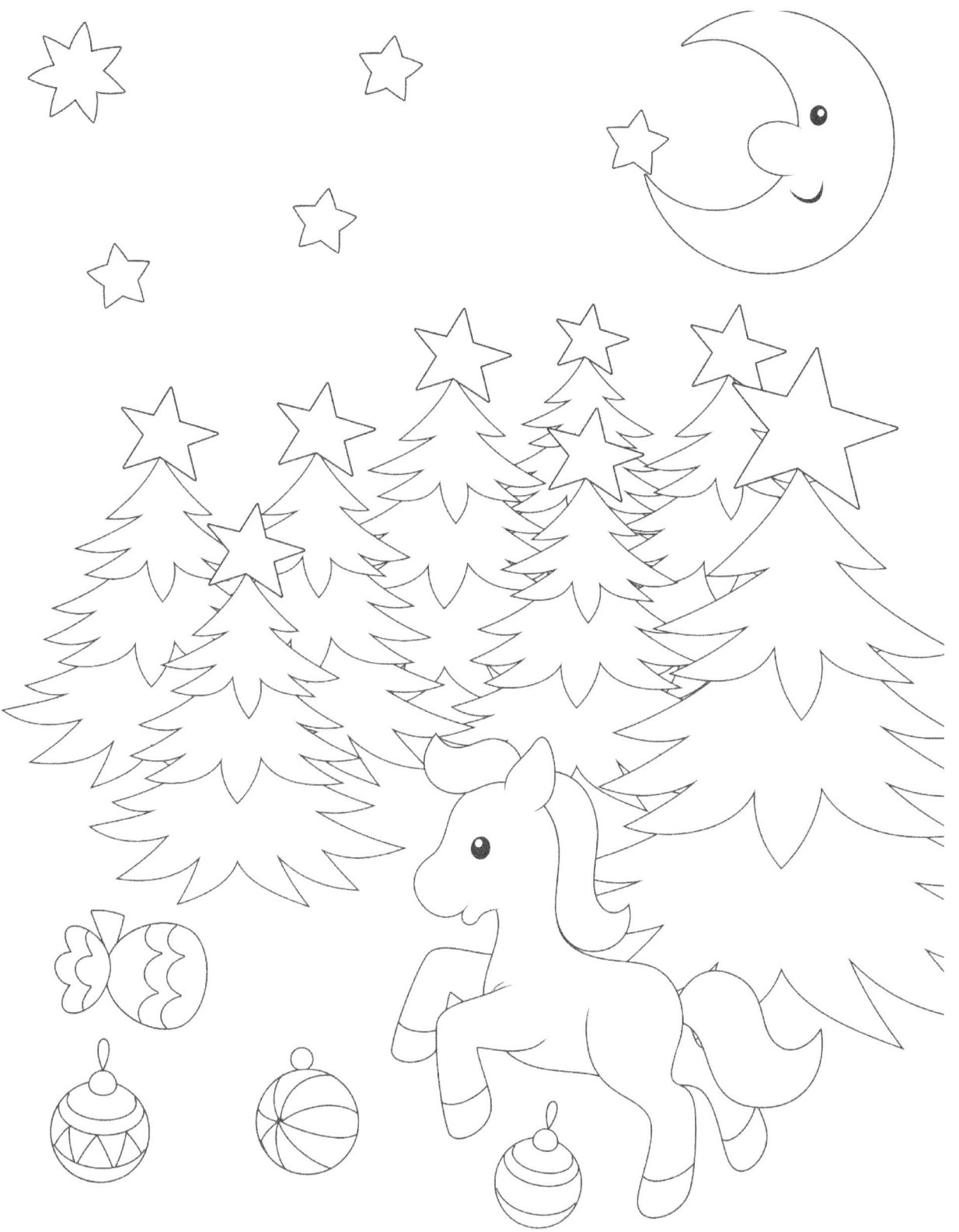

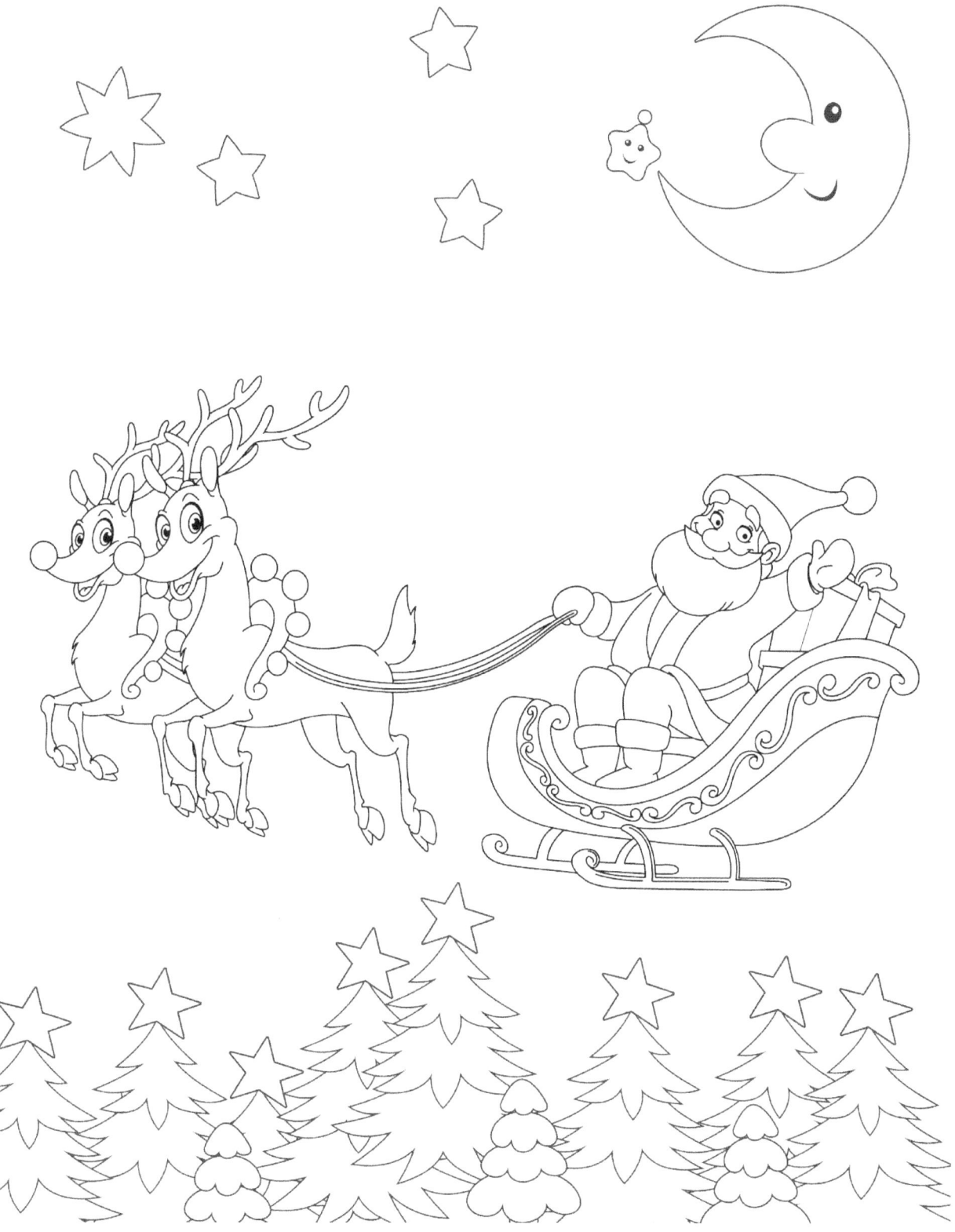

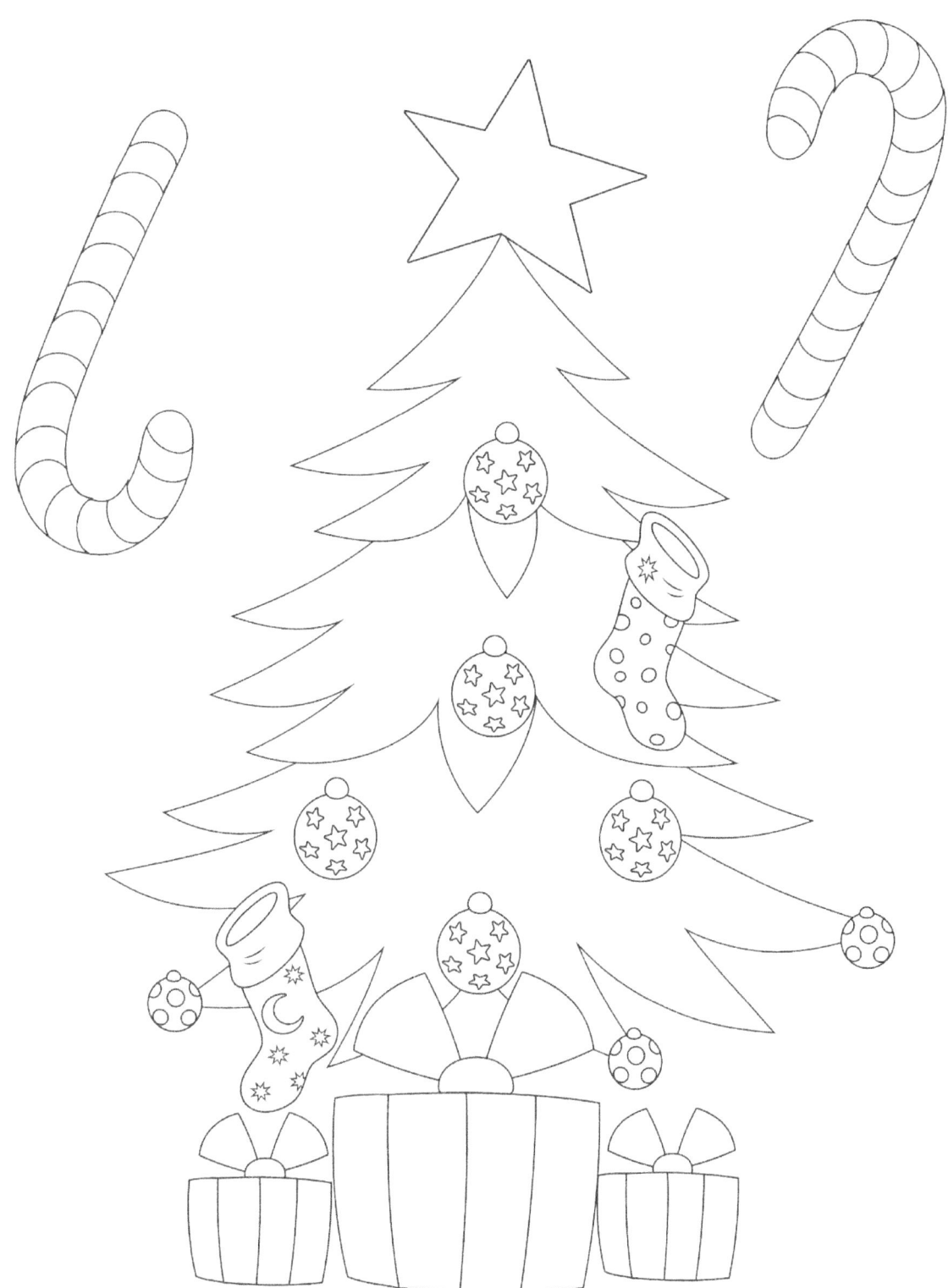

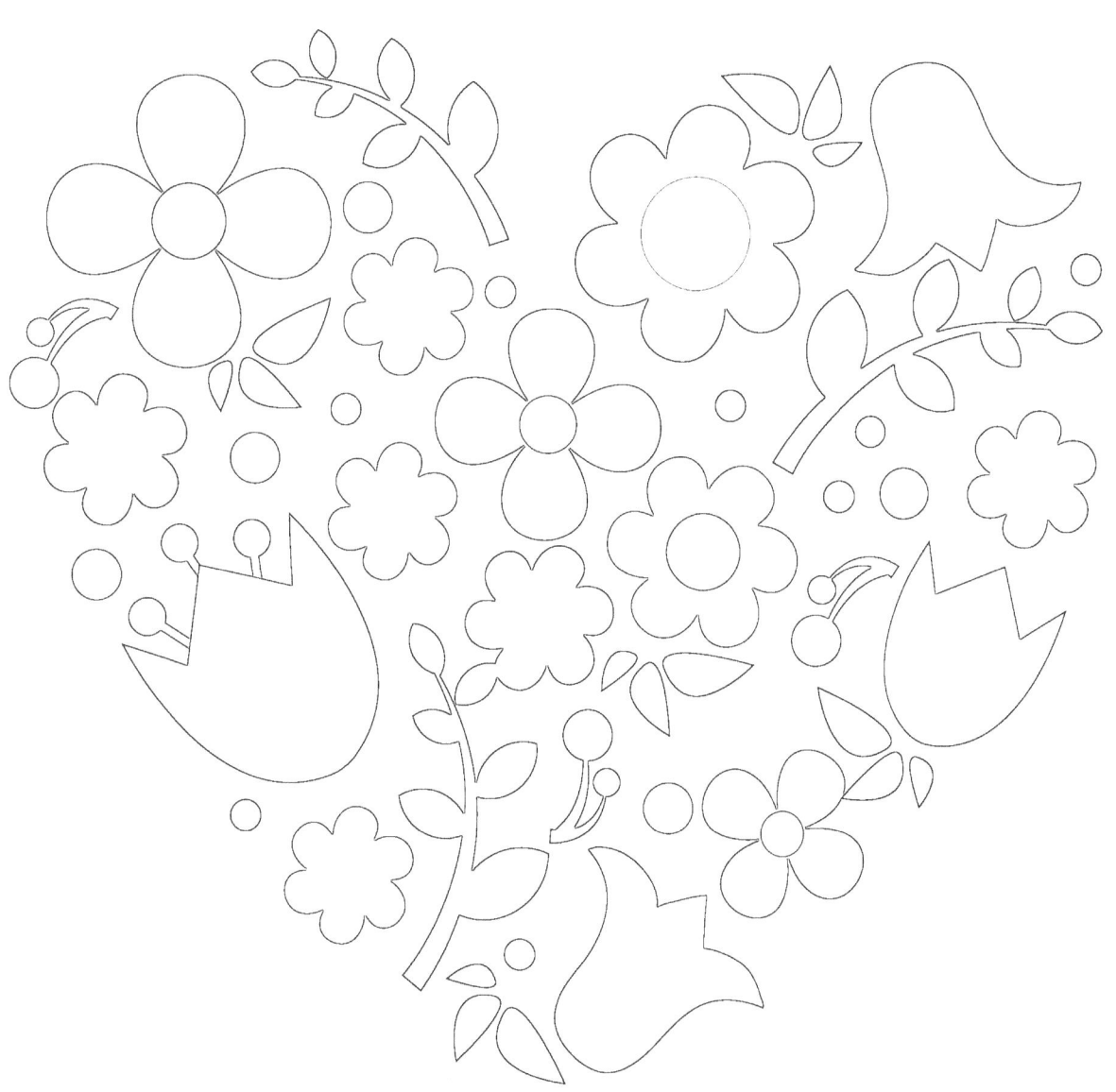

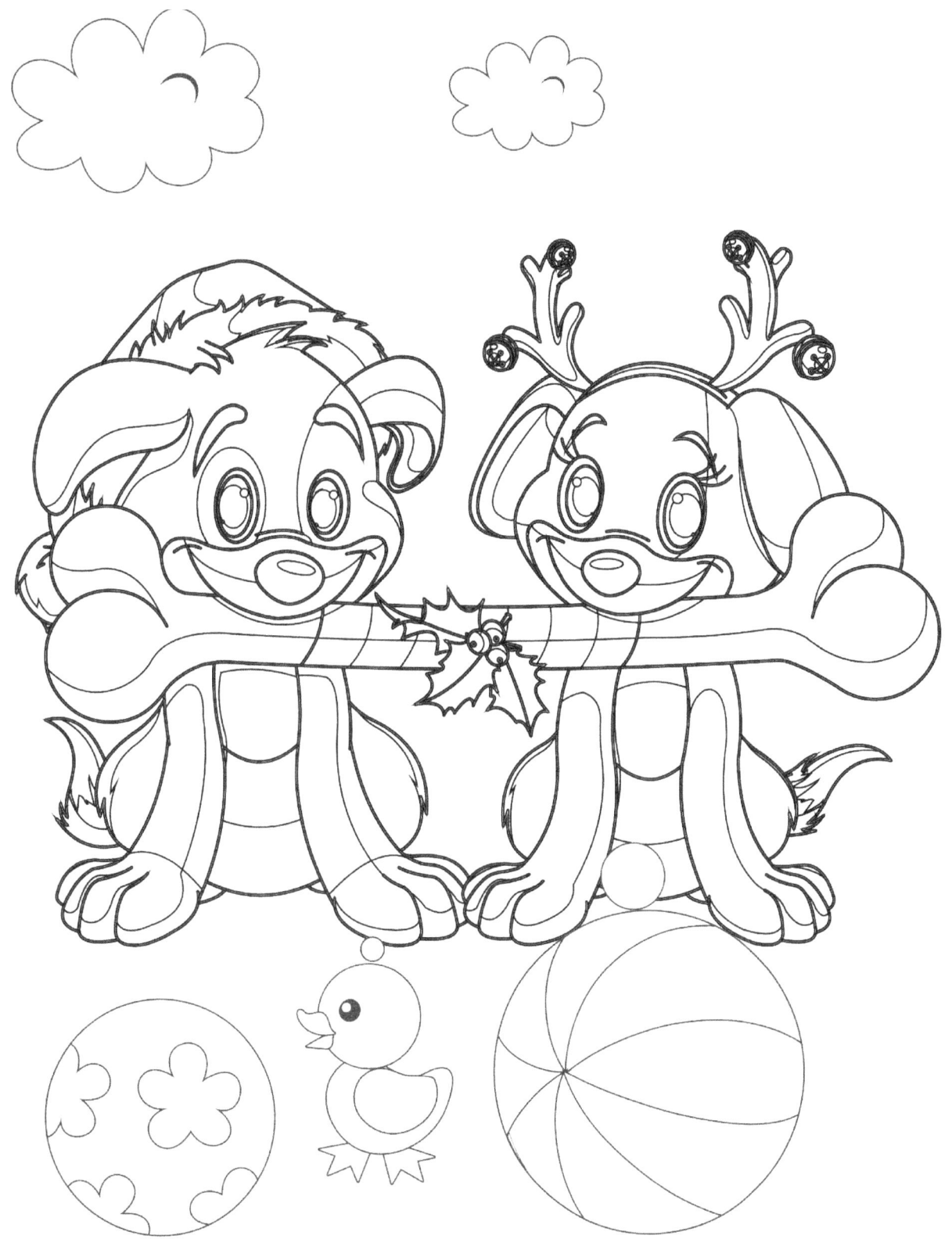

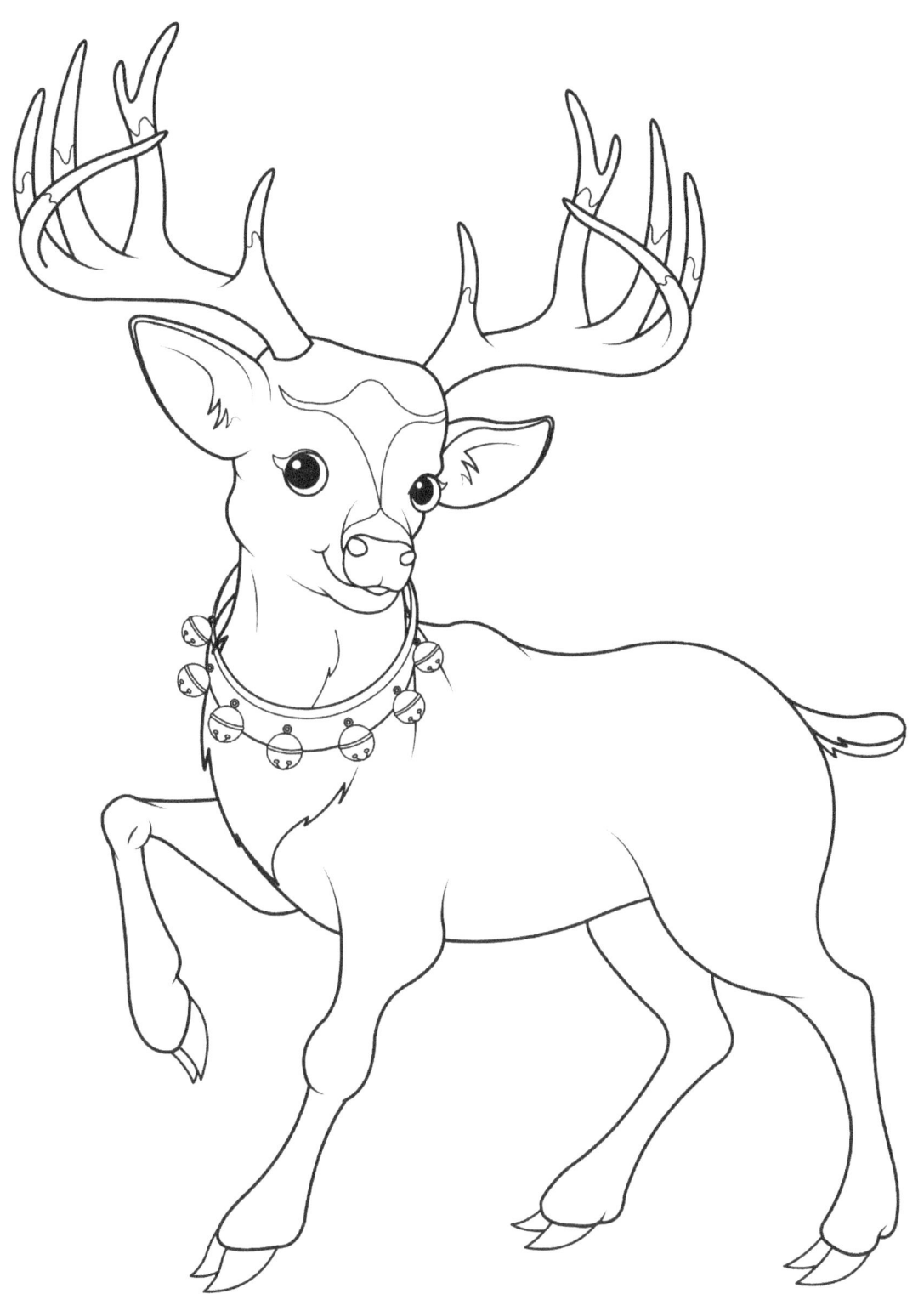

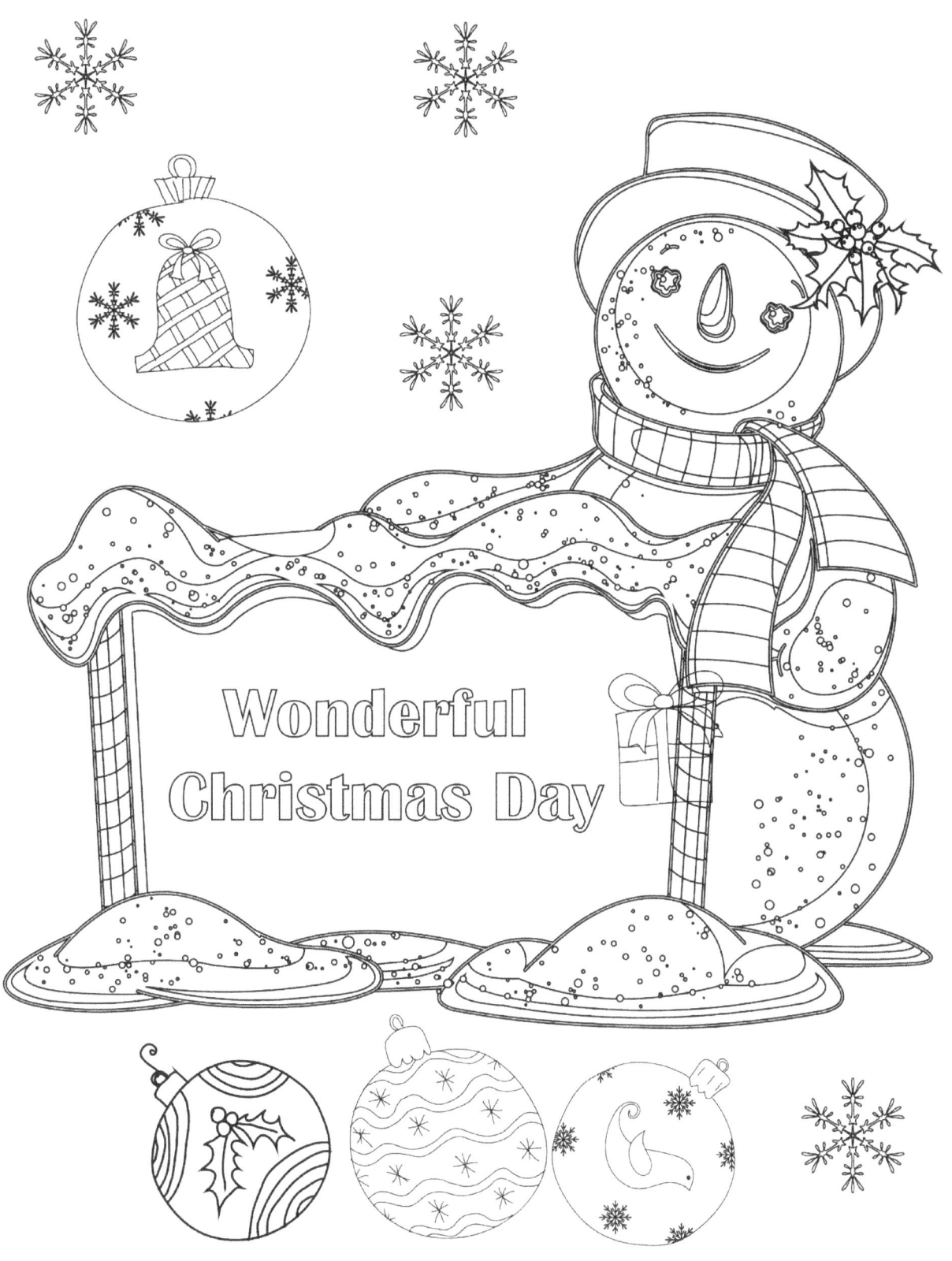

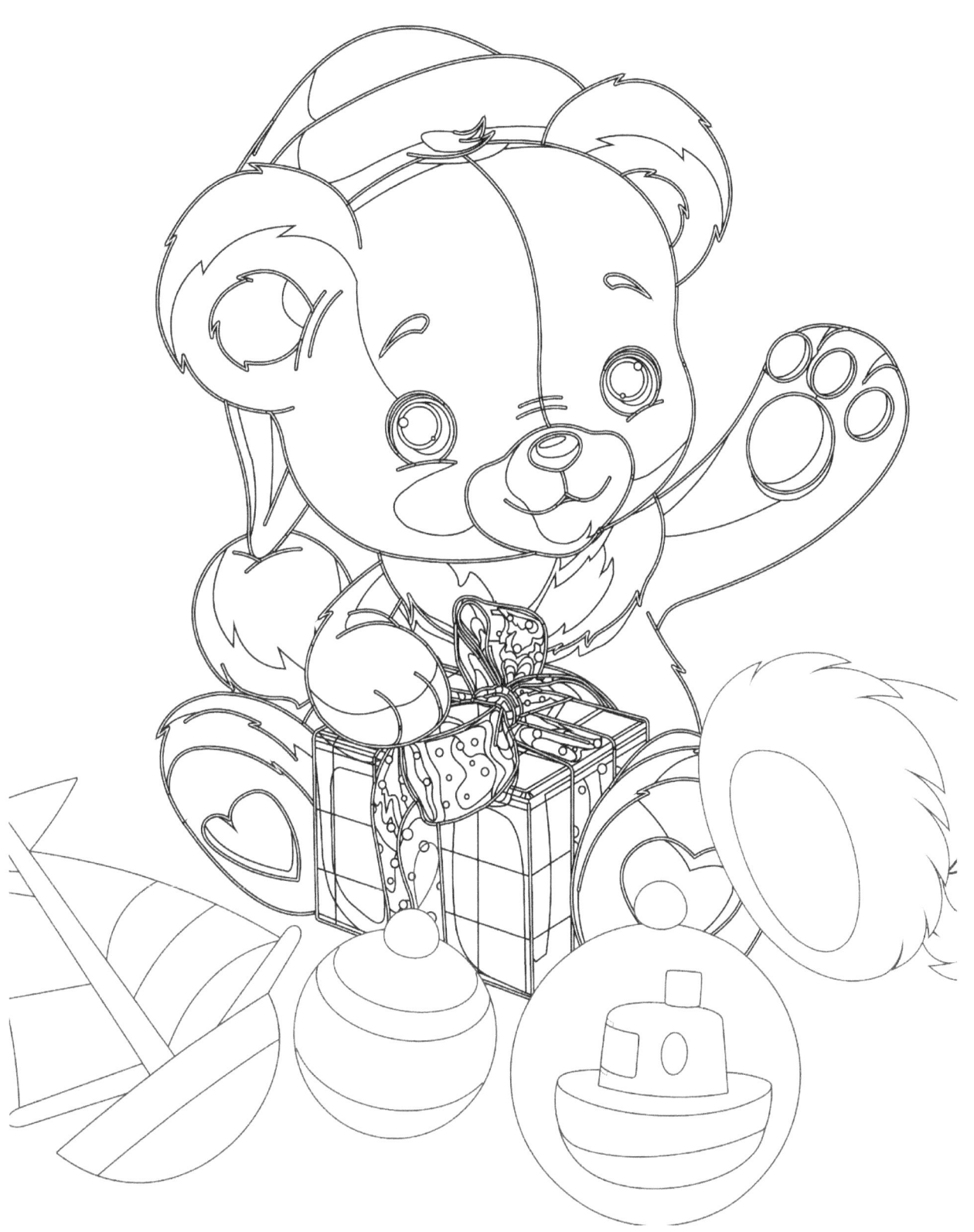

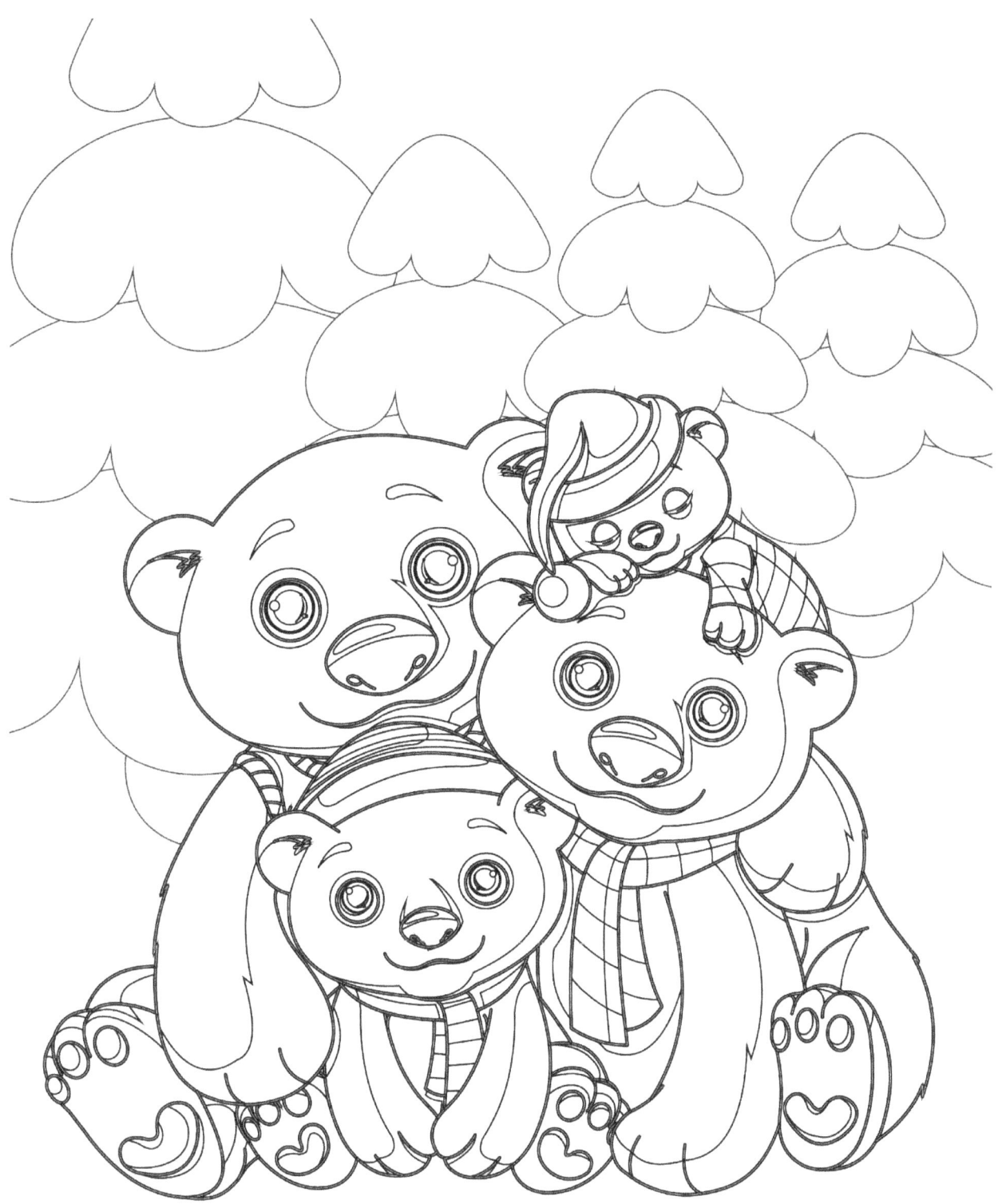

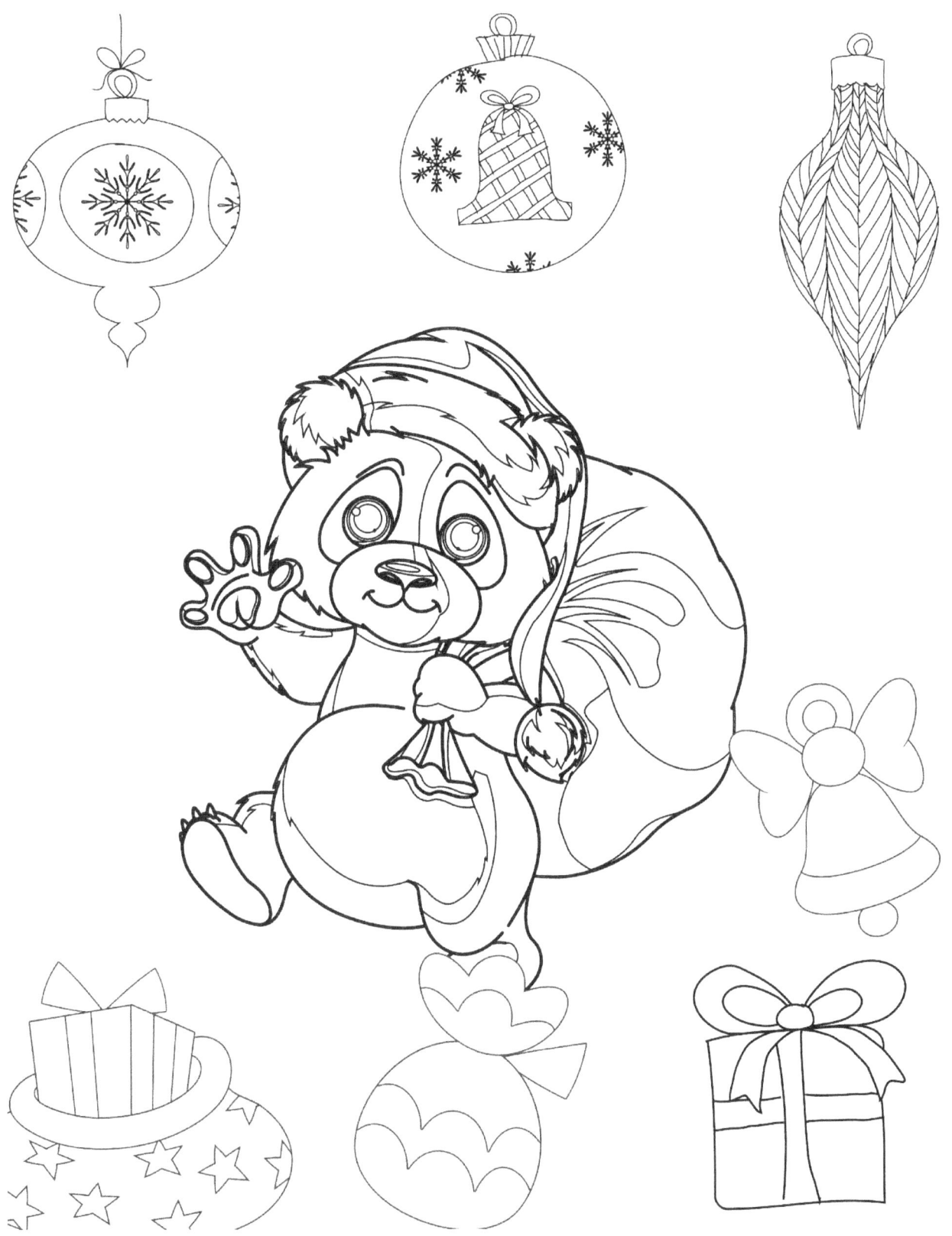

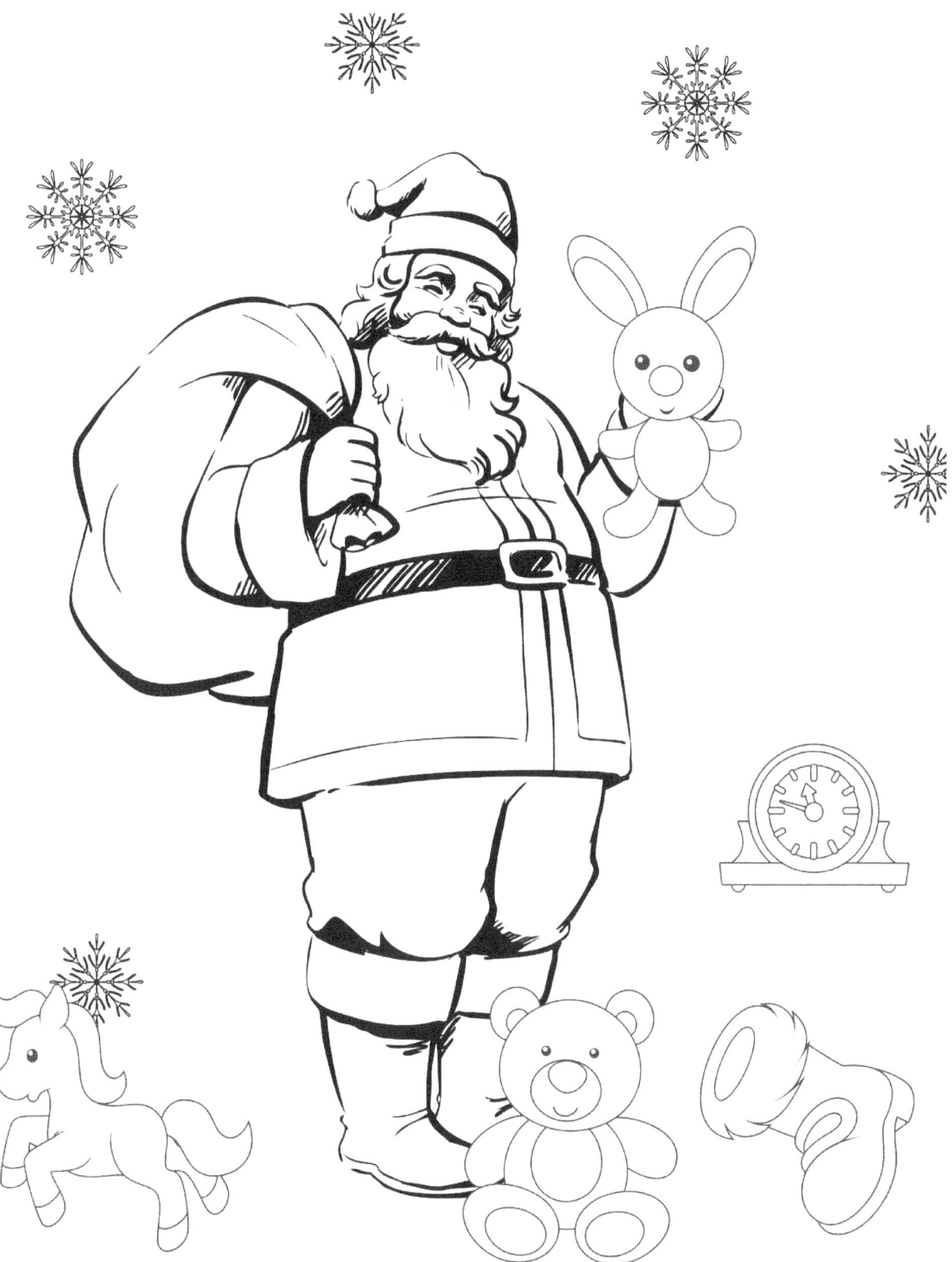

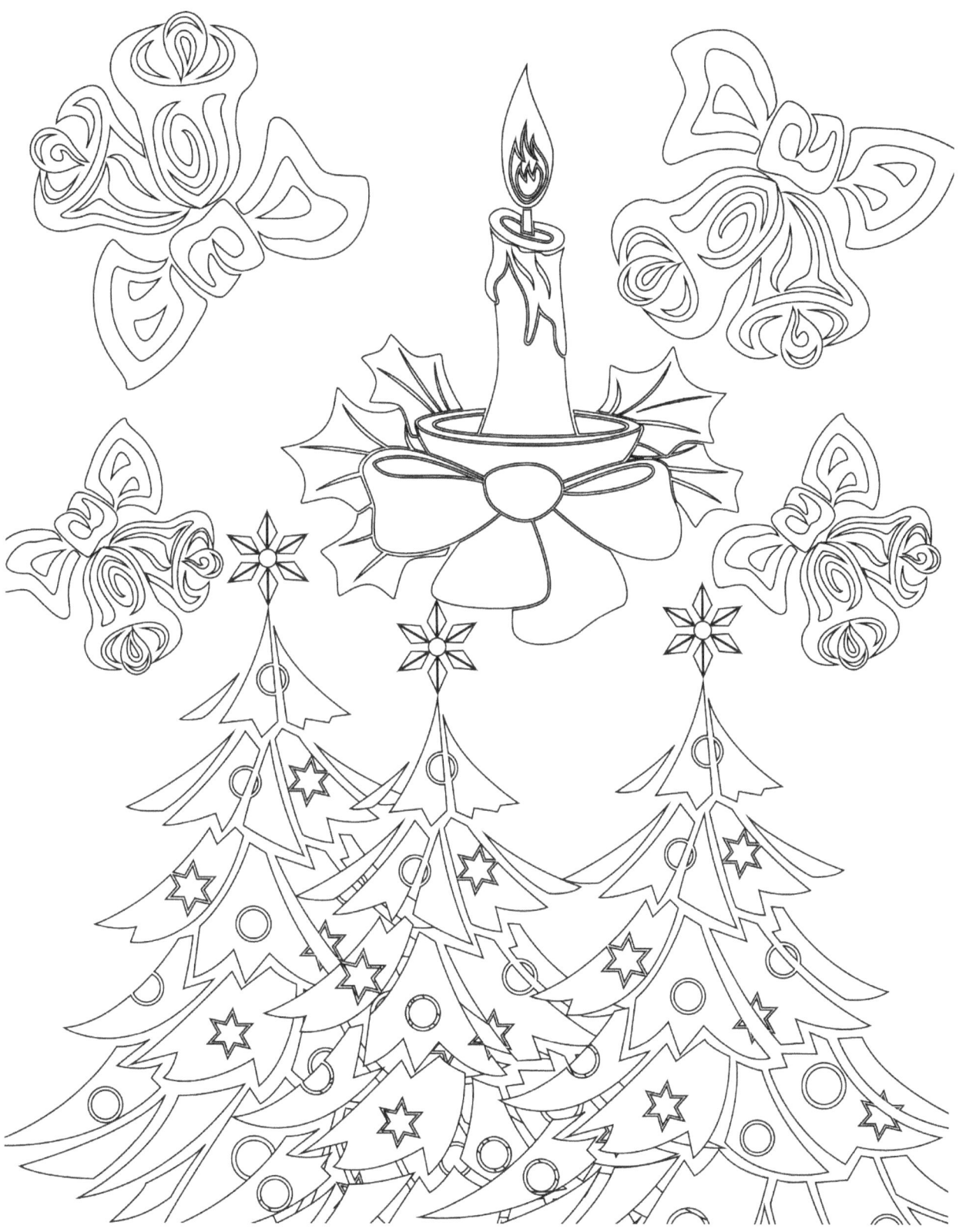

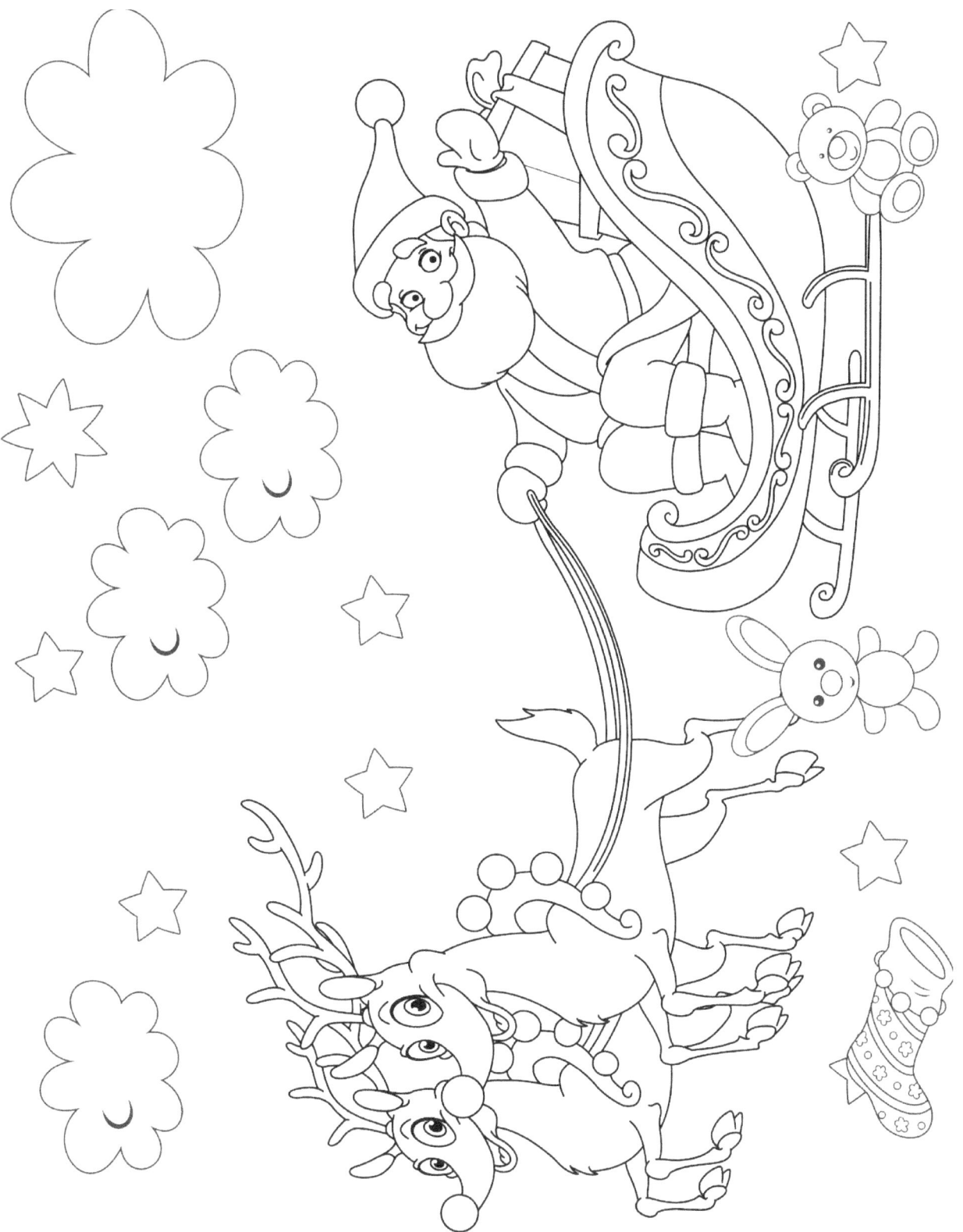